5 Levels of Praise Dance

MW01292752

Copyright 2015 - Wendy Bellonm

Contents

<u>Preface</u>

The Lord first gave me this teaching two and a half years ago. I believed in my heart that He wanted me to give it in a conference. So I stepped out in faith and taught it a mini dance workshop. I do love speaking but I found when I spoke it, it did not have a big of an impact as when I read my notes. For a while God has been urging me to write this down into a formal booklet. I was like "Who me? Write a book? Me? A writer? Naaah!!!" Throughout my entire life, however, I have always been able to communicate better through letters, emails and eventual text messaging that I can face to face or over the phone. I always received one of the highest grades in class when it came to term papers. The Lord was bringing up all these memories from school and I still battled the idea of a book. The word itself was just so intimidating. I thought it would be too difficult and I would write two pages and run out of things to say.

Once I began, my fingers went into this typing frenzy. The only reason I would stop was because I would get really hungry, and it was weird because it felt like I had been writing for five minutes when in reality it was actually five hours. Why do we fight with God? Why do we constantly try to tell Him what we need, when He is the one who knows us best? We tell Him what we think we can and cannot do, when He knows it all?

The "5 Levels of Praise Dance" is a journey through the bible by studying different dancers and what we can learn from them to grow in our own ministry. We will look at more known dancers like Miriam and of course David. Some less studied characters like Jephthah's daughter, Michal, Salome and Prochorus. It is an in-depth bible study on the good and the bad of dance in the bible. God gives us examples on what He desires praise to be and also bad examples to avoid in our dance ministries. I have also included some personal testimonial stories. I believe that there is a lot to learn from listening about another's life and how they were able to overcome certain situations.

I pray that this book blesses you and your ministry and that the Lord may speak to you and may inspire you to grow as a dancer for Him. We were born for such a time as this. In these last days, God is trying to awaken His church and trying to bring dance back into worship where it belongs. Lets rise up and answer that calling!

Level 1
Miriam

And Miriam the prophetess, the sister of Aaron, took a timbrel in her hand; and all the women went out after her with timbrels and with dances. Ex 15:20 NKJV

Interestingly enough Miriam is referred to as a prophetess. A prophet is a person who speaks for God by divine inspiration; or a person chosen to speak for God *(3)*. She was a person who danced for God by divine inspiration; She was a person chosen to dance for God. That is what this first level is about, a calling upon your life. I love how the first account in dance we encounter in the bible is described as prophetic. God is telling us from the get-go that our dances to Him should be divinely inspired and we should be chosen to dance. Miriam was not called a prophetess until after she danced.

In the scriptures only six women have been called a prophetess.

Old Testament

>   Miriam *(Ex 15:20)*

>   Deborah *(Judges 4:4)*

>   Huldah *(2 Kings 22:14)*

>   Noadiah *(Neh 6:14)*

>   Isaiahs Wife *(Is 8:3)*

New Testament

>   Anna *(Luke 2:36)*

Prophets were once called seer's *(1 Samuel 9:9)*, because God gives him or her the gift of foreknowledge or an awareness of something before it happens or exists. We should see the dance God wants us to do before ever stepping foot in rehearsal, much less on a stage. It is not random movements; that is what a performance is. A true minister of dance will enter into Gods presence and receive the message He wants delivered to His people. True prophesy comes only by the Holy Spirit *(2 Peter 1:21)*. It is the Holy Spirit who will put a message in your heart. Before you begin choosing your song, invite the Holy Spirit to listen in with you and He will tell you which song He wants you to dance to. You could find some beautiful songs but you will sense the spirit say "no" because that is not the message that He wants to deliver. Once the spirit approves of a song, the choreography will begin to flow naturally. As if the spirit that resides in you had already choreographed it and just needed a body to use.

Not only does the spirit choose music and choreography but He will also inspire wardrobe. Colors have biblical meaning. Let's say that God gave you a song about covenant, but you decide you want to wear black and red. Black signifies death and red signifies the blood of Jesus. That mixture of these colors represents sacrifice not covenant. After the deluge in Genesis, God put a rainbow in the sky as a covenant to never destroy humanity in the same fashion. God used six colors to represent a covenant, so would it not be more fitting to wear the six colors of the rainbow?

I challenge everyone reading this to try this: do a dance with your choice of wardrobe, a month or two later do the exact same dance in the colors that match the message of the dance. Compare the two experiences and notice the difference in the deliverance of the message. Our dancing is not a performance and it is not entertainment. It is a message! It should be just as powerful as any preaching. The same goes for the ministry of singing or acting because it is not a filler in a service, it is part of worship and it should bless someone spiritually. Sometimes when I dance I see the audiences faces and they all look like they have been chloroformed, except for this one person with tears in their eyes in the corner. That dance was solely meant for one person. God loves us so much that He will make a person go through weeks and months of rehearsal just to reach you and choreograph a dance just for you. Other times I have danced, the audience is at an uproar and you can hear the movement of God in the room. You can actually feel the same spirit dwelling between you and the audience. One of these is not better than the other. Both these scenarios are important to God and should therefore be equally important to you. As humans, we prefer the latter scenario because it makes us feel worthy, and supported. That can be very dangerous because the hooting and hollering are not directed towards us. It is the movement of God that has caused such a beautiful atmosphere, not the movement of our body.

Miriam danced in gratitude. Out of the joy in her heart, she begins to worship and praise the Lord. Her attitude of praise influenced other women to join in and praise along with her. As dancers we should also inspire others to praise. We do not just move for entertainment. Our worship should be contagious. However, she had a problem with gossip. In the book of Numbers, chapter12, we learn that she had a problem with the woman Moses took for a wife and spoke badly about them. God called all three of them to His presence and reprimanded her for speaking against one of His prophets. He struck her with leprosy and she had to reside outside of the camp until she was healed. Miriam let her head get big and began to gossip about her fellow teammates. We cannot let ourselves begin to gossip about our teammates, or God might just strike us with a spiritual leprosy in our finances, family, or work.

For I brought you up from the land of Egypt, I redeemed you from the house

of bondage; And I sent before you Moses, Aaron, and Miriam. Micha 6:4

Miriam was not just the older sister of Aaron and Moses. God used all three siblings to lead the people of Israel. God did not care that she was a woman. In his eyes, all three of them were prophets. She betrayed someone in her group, in her team, and in her ministry. I have danced in both church and have been technically trained in the secular world. I have seen groups torn apart because of gossip and cliques. If you are not united, your teams will crumble to nothing. Do not let petty things come between each other. I believed my past teammates were my friends only to find out that they were saying things about me that were not very nice. Comments would get back to me that I danced too hard and that I looked ridiculous. Some of them would actually laugh when I would start dancing and tell me I looked really bad. These were not random audience members, these were my teammates. I would feel so bad and convince myself that dance just was not my calling. I would have people come up to me and tell me that I moved them and that I truly have a gift. I was so confused because I really wanted to believe that my teammates had my best interest in mind. I eventually left that group and continued dancing by myself. Once I did that, God really started working in my life through dance, but we must realize that it is God who dances through us.

Pipes deliver water to our houses but the pipes are only a means of delivering the water. There is a main power plant that cleanses the water and decides where to send it. The pipeline is only an instrument designed for a specific area. The pipelines in my house only deliver water to my house. They cannot deliver water to someone who lives in New York. We are like pipelines; we are just instruments. God is the main power plant and the water is His Holy Spirit. God decides where to send the water and uses the pipelines to deliver His message. But a pipeline cannot deliver water if it is not connected to the main source or if it is broken. We must stay connect to the main source; we must stay connect to God. We cannot expect to minister or bless others through dance when we are living a life of sin behind closed doors. Maybe we are not living in sin but we are not consecrating ourselves to God either.

Level 2

Jephthah's Daughter

And Jephthah made a vow to the Lord, and said, "If You will indeed deliver the people of Ammon into my hands, then it will be that whatever comes out of the doors of my house to meet me, when I return in peace from the people of Ammon, shall surely be the Lord's, and I will offer it up as a burnt offering." ...When Jephthah came to his house at Mizpah, there was his daughter, coming out to meet him with timbrels and dancing; and she was his only child. Besides her he had neither son nor daughter. And it came to pass, when he saw her, that he tore his clothes, and said, "Alas, my daughter! You have brought me very low! You are among those who trouble me! For I have given my word to the Lord, and I cannot go back on it." So she said to him, "My father, if you have given your word to the Lord, do to me according to what has gone out of your mouth, because the Lord has avenged you of your enemies, the people of Ammon."

Judges 11:30-31, 34-36 NKJV

Now I am not saying that we should light up our grills and go
nap on them. Jephthahs daughter represents sacrifice. The burnt
offering alter was made of acacia wood and plated in bronze. As
soon as you would enter through the gates of the tabernacle, the first
furnishing you would encounter was The Alter of Burnt Offerings.
The Psalmist wrote enter through his gates with thanksgiving. That
is what Miriam did as she danced in thanksgiving when God
destroyed the Egyptians in the red sea. After entering His gates with
thanksgiving we are ready to give our burnt offering. Like I
mentioned in the last chapter, the Lord began to work in my life
through dance. It was not due to leaving my previous group; it was
due to consecrating me to Him.

I began to detach myself from the secular world and latch on
to God's will for my life. I began to pray daily, and I am not talking
about saying grace and bed prayers; I am talking about all day
meditation on God. As I ate lunch, I turned off all appliances and
gave grace like I normally would but once I started eating I began
talking to Him about how my day was going. Granted, I am sure

others thought as I was insane because I would also do this in public. Sometimes, I would make a joke and I would feel Him make a joke back. I finally understood what Abraham said when he said that he was friends with God. I developed such a beautiful friendship with Him. I began to fall so deeply in love with Jesus that I wanted to know more about Him. I began to read the scriptures on my own time, instead of just opening it once a week at church. It was like God's biography; He was the main character and God would fill me with His spirit. A story that would have seemed trivial a few months ago, all the sudden held so much revelation that it would move me to tears. I wanted more and wanted to connect at a deeper level. I began to fast regularly and that was not easy. I am such a foodie; I love food so much but God meant more to me than food. I would wake up at six in the morning on my day off, excited to spend my entire morning and part of my afternoon giving undivided attention to my savior.

I was not searching for dance and it was not about my ministry. It was about developing my love story with someone who loved me so much that He died for me. The Lord began to share with me His vision for my life. He gave me two prophetic words from two separate pastors who did not know each other; and the crazy thing is that they both said the same thing. God began to show me dances in my head. Unexplainably, the Lord brought yards of free fabric in my hands and gave me the designs for dancewear. He began to inspire conferences and book ideas. My ministry took off like a rocket, spiritually, because things must happen in the spiritual world before they can manifest themselves in the material world. Though I was still dancing alone, I was never lonely. The Lord allowed hardships in my life but through them, I was able to understand true worship through dance.

Jephthahs daughters' response was so amazing; she said "My father, if you have given your word to the Lord, do to me according to what has gone out of your mouth". She did not throw a tantrum or disrespect her father by saying "how could you be so stupid? You're ruining my life!!" She accepted to be given as a sacrifice without batting an eyelash. It was not a chore or a burden. She gave herself up as a sacrifice for the love of her father and gratitude towards the Lord. She understood that you cannot back out of the promises we make to God. She gladly gave herself in sacrifice. That is how we should also approach the thought of giving ourselves to God.

Sacrifice has such a negative connotation attached to it. What is so wrong about sacrificing our single life to marry someone wonderful God has blessed us with? What is wrong about sacrificing your body and sleep to take care of a defenseless newborn? Or sacrificing some of your Friday nights to study instead of going out to dinner yet again? These are good sacrifices, these are burdens we take on happily because they are not as heavy as many seem to think they are. The sacrifice of consecrating yourself to Christ is the best burden you could ever carry because it is so light.

Come to Me, all you who labor and are heavy laden, and I will give you rest.

Take My yoke upon you and learn from Me, for I am gentle and lowly in heart,

and you will find rest for your souls. For My yoke is easy and My burden is light.

Matthew 11: 28-30 NKJV

Sacrifice is required for cleansing. In a burnt offering the fire (Holy Spirit) consumed everything and the animal brought to be sacrificed was of the highest quality. We cannot read a biblical chapter a week, have timed prayers, fast once a year and expect the world in return. Our sacrifice has to be of the highest quality. I encourage you to read the scriptures daily, to get so lost in conversation with God that you lose track of time, and experience the joy of giving Jesus undivided attention.

One of the most interesting things about Jephthahs daughter is that her name is never given. Who she was did not matter; the only thing we see is her sacrifice and her dance. When you dance, you should strive to be nameless. You no longer exist when you minister. You are the pipeline behind the wall that one sees. When the faucet is turned on, people just want the water. No one is interested in the dirty old pipe that is used to deliver the water. When people go to church, they do not go for you and me. They are not interested in what we have to offer. They are only interested in the rivers of living water that the Lord has to offer. Right before any dance that I do, my only prayer is "Thank you Lord for this opportunity that you have granted me to dance for your people, but I do not exist. I do not want to exist. All I want is to be an instrument for you to flow through. Dance with me, be my dance partner and may this worship be pleasing in your sight. Amen"

Level 3
David

And David danced before the Lord with all his might;

and David was girded with a linen ephod. 2 Sam 6:14 NKJV

Thus all Israel brought up the ark of the covenant of the Lord

with shouting and with the sound of the horn, with trumpets and with

cymbals, making music with stringed instruments and harps. 1

Chron 15:28 NKJV

David is the most known dancer in the scriptures and with

good reason. There is so much that can be learned from David's

worship. David was, above all else, a worshipper; He was a

worshipper before he was a king, a father, or husband. In his time

with God, he always gave his all and he never gave anything less

than his best. I have seen so many dancers, in group and

individually, who look like they rehearsed for weeks and months but fail to worship while they dance. They are focused on movement and choreography. The point of rehearsal is so that when it comes time to participate, you can let your muscles worry about the memorization of the steps and you are free to enter into worship. If you are not allowing yourself to be ministered to, how do you expect God to use you to minister through?

Our goal is to take people into the presence of God. How can we lead someone to a place we have never been before? What if I told you that there was this amazing, wonderful place where all your dreams come true? Your reaction would be to ask for directions and how you can get to this wonderful place. However, I do not actually know how to get there so I tell you "just drive north for four hours and you should see it on your right". Those are not very reliable directions. We need to know how to enter into God's presence. When we dance before an audience, God is giving us a steering wheel and telling us to take them into His presence. But if you do not know how to get there, how can you take anyone else there? You know those "Rico Suave" types of guys who think they are God's gift to women and expect all women to swoon at their feet? As ministers, we have to be careful not to turn into a spiritual "Rico Suave". A type of person that just expects to touch people's hearts, cause teary eyes, and have the whole auditorium to be slain in the spirit just because you are the one dancing. Dancing whole heartedly and showing off are not synonyms.

We have to examine our hearts for weeks before we ever step foot on a stage. Figure out the reason why you are doing what you are doing. It is so easy to proclaim some lame, vague, expected, Sunday school answer like "Well, I want to minister and I love to praise God. The bible says we should dance for Him and this is my calling. There are different ways to worship God and people should worship with us as we dance". This type of response is not wrong, just superficial. Why do you want to minister? Why do you love to praise God? Why is it your calling? Why?! Do not answer these questions with more vague answers. Like: The bible says we should minister; I love to praise God because the bible says he is x, y, z; It is my calling because I am a leader. Superficial! Your answers should be nothing short than personal.

I used to give vague answers as well, not really knowing why I danced. God used dance to help me through a point in my life when everything had gone bananas. My whole world turned upside down and it was so difficult to even want to wake up in the morning because everything was a mess. I would listen to worship music that spoke to my situation and I began to dance by myself in my room. I was not trying to impress anyone, I was not trying to choreograph, and there was no intension of rehearsal. As I prayed, I would just move wherever my spirit took me. My emotions were being released through movement. It was like I was having a conversation with Christ. The movement became a prayer that only He and I understood. For months I danced for the Lord with no intention of doing it in front of anyone. Then one day, He spoke to me and put a song in my heart, movement in my body, and told me to ask for participation. It was my first solo and when that day arrived I was (literally) shaking in my (figurative)boots. As the music began, I felt Christ say "There's no one here, it is just you and Me". My nerves went away and instead of dancing, I began to converse with my Lord. There, in front of my entire youth church, something interesting happened; through my movement, the Lord began to speak to those watching and they were transported into the presence of God because I made the decision to go there first. I have heard so many people say "It was hard to get into the song because the crowd was so dead". You are up there as a worship leader; it is your responsibility to lead them into worship not the other way around.

So they carried the ark of God on a new cart from the house of

Abinadab, and

Uzza and Ahio drove the cart...And when they came to Chidon's

threshing floor,

Uzza put out his hand to hold the ark, for the oxen stumbled. Then

the anger of the

Lord was aroused against Uzza, and He struck him because he put

his hand to the ark;

and he died there before God. 1 Chron 13:7, 9-10 NKJV

David thought that his good intensions would be enough, but it was not. David was so scared after this incident that he left the ark in the house Obed-edom for three months and then educated himself on how to properly transport it. We have little to no respect for the things of God and hold recitals at church instead of intention of ministering. Dancing is so much fun but it is my ministry not my hobby. I just happen to find joy in my ministry. It is not about having the "coolest movement" or being the best dance group. There is no thought into what we do and we move without fully understanding why we do what we do. For a long time I did not understand Uzza's death. Uzza saw the oxen stumble and his first reaction was to protect the Ark of the Covenant from falling to the floor. Uzza had good intentions but ultimately showed a lack of respect for God, all things pertaining to God and a disobedience to His commandants. In those things there is no blessing. Uzza's actual death is symbolic to us; we spiritually die when we no longer fear God and disobey his commandments.

And it was so, that when they that bare the ark of the Lord had gone

six paces,

he sacrificed oxen and fatlings. And David danced before the Lord

with all his might;

and David was girded with a linen ephod.So David and all the house

of Israel brought up

the ark of the Lord with shouting, and with the sound of the trumpet.

2 Sam 6:13-15 NKJV

From the house of Obed-edom all the way back to the city, David walked six steps, offered a sacrifice to the Lord and then David danced with all his might. Even if, hypothetically speaking, Obed-edom's house was only a mile away from the city, do you know how long it would take to only go six steps, stop, sacrifice an animal, and worship in song and dance; then take another six steps, stop, sacrifice an animal, and worship in song and dance; and again six more steps, stop, sacrifice an animal, and worship in song and dance; Over and over and over again until they reached the city? David danced with all his might way before he danced in front the entire kingdom. He only allowed himself to travel six steps before offering another sacrifice and dancing before the Lord. We think that attending dance rehearsal is sacrifice enough and then wonder why there is no difference in the atmosphere after we participate. Yes, it is true that God is love and He will protect us and provide for us but we cannot forget that God is also all powerful. We need to learn to fear the Lord and understand that we serve a great God. There is little respect for God's presence these days. David learned the hard way to fear the Lord.

David is considered a role model because he danced with all his might and he inspired an entire kingdom to worship God in a new way. We forget, however, the lesson he had to learn and steps he had to follow in order to be that role model. We want to be that role model but want to take shortcuts to get there. There is so much more we have to learn and steps we have to follow in order to reach

this level and to be like David.

Level 4
Michal

And it happened, as the ark of the covenant of the Lord came to the

City of David,

that Michal, Saul's daughter, looked through a window and saw

King David whirling

and playing music; and she despised him in her heart. 1 Chron 15:29

nkjv

Then David returned to bless his household. And Michal the

daughter of Saul came

out to meet David, and said, How glorious was the king of Israel to

day, who

uncovered himself to day in the eyes of the handmaids of his

servants, as one of the

vain fellows shamelessly uncovereth himself! And David said unto

Michal, It was

before the Lord, which chose me before thy father, and before all his

house, to appoint me ruler over the people of the Lord, over Israel:

therefore will I play before the Lord. And I will yet be more vile than

thus, and will be base in mine own sight:

and of the maidservants which thou hast spoken of, of them shall I be

had in honour.

2 Sam 6:20-22 NKJV

Oh Michal! What a character! Michal represents those Christians that do not believe in dance in the church. Those whose comments destroy instead of build up. You would think that David's own wife would be supportive of his ministry. It goes to show that those who we thought were our friends and who we thought were close to us, will speak badly of us even if what we do is pleasing in God's sight. How sad is it that the Lord rejoices in our dance but we do not meet the standards of certain Christians?

Every praise dancer will encounter a Michal or sometimes even more than one. A Michal is not someone who simply just speaks badly towards the ministry. It is someone who you thought would support you and instead is running your name through the mud. It could be a friend, a relative, or a leader that completely discourages you dancing before the Lord and even refuses to believe that anyone was ever touched through your dance, despite the evidence.

Once upon a time, similar words were said about me and towards me:

--"Wendy's dancing too hard, it looks weird."

--"Your dancing is standing out and it looks bad because the rest of us are not dancing like that."

--*One of them laughed as we watch one of our videos* "Ew look at Wendy! We told you stop doing that because it does not look good"

--*Overheard someone giving group members a compliment* "You guys did awesome! You guys are really good....but Wendy? She is on another level! She makes me feel the music. You should all dance that hard." *Their response* "Why does everyone keep saying that? She is not even that good!"

That really hurt my feelings. This was my team; we were supposed to be encouraging one another not putting each other down. You are going to get enough grief from the church elders that are not used to having dance as part of their worship; the last thing you need or want is to start turning on each other. I never "corrected" my "mistake" of standing out because I danced way too hard and the bullying, for lack of a better word, continued and got worse overtime. The Lord has been with me and brought me out of so much garbage that life and the enemy have thrown my way. I am not going to restrain my worship just because someone does not feel like praising God with all that they have. I cannot hold my praise back just because someone does not agree with my form of worship. Needless to say, I did not last for long in that group and was eventually replaced. Afterwards, I did not dance for about two years; being stabbed figuratively is much more painful than being stabbed literally.

In modern terms, David told his wife: "It was God who chose me to be king; therefore I will play before the Lord. And I will dance and shout and sing even harder and louder that what I was just doing! Oh, and those people you were taking about, they did not think I was acting foolishly like you claimed. They rejoice along with me!" David was unapologetic for his praise and worship. Never dull your shine just because someone does not want you to shine brighter than them. Do not think that just because he had this epic comeback that his feelings were not hurt. Just because it seems like someone's feelings were not hurt by your words does not mean it is true. However, if you have been hurt you have to learn to draw strength from the Lord and rise above those comments. As much as those words hurt, continue praising the Lord with all your heart, mind and strength.

You will have Michal's in your ministry and you are going to have to develop a thick skin because the higher you go in ministry, the meaner the comments get. You cannot rely on the praise of others to encourage you in ministry. One negative word can and will bring it all down. Now a day, people care more about what their peers think and climbing the ministry ladder than they do about pleasing the Lord. If I had a dollar every time someone said something negative about my ministry, I could retire tomorrow. However! Having a Michal in your life is not the same as someone trying to give you a legitimate correction so that you can better yourself as a dancer.

Whoever loves discipline loves knowledge,

but whoever hates correction is stupid.

Pro 12:1 NIV

Whoever stubbornly refuses to accept criticism

will suddenly be destroyed beyond recovery.

What Michal did was not criticism, it was pompous and condescending. There is such a thing as improper movement in the praise dance, but just because it is new or different does not make it improper. Many people do not like change but the bible tells us to "sing a new song unto the Lord". The real translation of sing and song in this verse is actually praise. So, the Hebrew version says "praise a new praise unto the Lord". Our praise should always be new and different and fresh. Do not let naysayers, which are trying to dull your shine, make you not want to dance again. We need to encourage ourselves in the Lord and realize that it is for Him who we dance for, and not for mans entertainment.

Level 5

Prochorus

And the saying pleased the whole multitude: and they chose Stephen,

a man full

of faith and of the Holy Ghost, and Philip, and **Prochorus***, and*

Nicanor, and Timon,

and Parmenas, and Nicolas a proselyte of Antioch: Acts 6:5 NKJV

Prochorus was one of the seven deacons chosen to serve in the church of Antioch. Interestingly enough, his name comes from the Latin language meaning: Pro=before, leader of, for; Chorus=dance, a round dance (2). His name literally means leader of dance. His actual duties are not recorded in scripture but I find it interesting that one the first leaders in the very first Christian church was called a leader of dance. Leadership is such a broad topic and there are even universities who offer minors in leadership. The best example of a leader is Jesus and he did not hold a man given title. He walked in the will of God and when you walk in the will of God, others will follow.

He who says he abides in Him ought himself also to walk just as He walked. 1 John 2:6

A true spiritual leader must have a burden to rebuild the church or in this case the dancers. Every leader must equipt his or her people with a tool for work, weapon for war and ear for spirit. Leadership is a process by which a person influences others to accomplish an objective and directs the organization in a way that makes it more cohesive and coherent. Power does not make you a leader; it simply makes you the boss. Leadership differs in that it makes the followers want to achieve high goals rather than feeling bossed around. Your challenge is to inspire people into higher levels of team work. The way in which you organize your ministry will determine in great manner how your vision unravels. The leader has to have communication with God that allows him or her to follow God's plan. The leaders goal is to direct the group into a complete surrender to God, an atmosphere of guidance and a passion to serve the Lord. Jesus was the ultimate leader; he is the perfect example of what true leadership is and what we must do to lead successfully.

We must become like Christ. We must follow his examples and, like Jesus, we must lead people into the light.

Jesus Led by Example

Be *"an example to the believers in word, in conduct, in love, in spirit, in faith, in purity..."* (1Tim 4:12). Jesus knew who He was and why He was here on this planet. Who are you and why are you here on Earth? Jesus based his life on fixed principles rather than making them up as he went along. So many leaders are like chameleons, changing their views to fit the situation. Jesus said several times "come follow me". He was more of a "do what I do" and not "do what I say". He led by example. Are you not being taken seriously as a leader? Do you fast? Do you pray? Do you read the bible? Do you take God seriously?

Jesus Was Selfless

For God so loved the world that He gave His only begotten Son, that whoever believes in Him should not perish but have everlasting life. John 3:16

This is My commandment, that you love one another as I have loved you.

Greater love has no one than this, than to lay down one's life for his friends.

John 15:12-13

Not only did He love but his love was beyond comprehension. As humans, it is very easy to become a selfish and manipulative leader; doing things not for a love of others but from a need to use them. These kinds of leaders focus on their own needs and desires, and not on the needs of others. Jesus was a selfless leader. Jesus involved His disciples; He gave them importance and gave them specific tasks. Many leaders try to do everything themselves, not allowing anyone else to grow; or worse not wanting others to grow in order to secure their position. Love cannot be hidden or suppressed, love always shines through. The ones you are leading will be able to tell if you truly care about them, about their spiritual life, about their ministry and not just yours.

Jesus was humble.

Everyone proud in heart is an abomination to the Lord;

Though they join forces, none will go unpunished.

Proverbs 16:5

Who say, 'Keep to yourself,

Do not come near me,

For I am holier than you!'

These are smoke in My nostrils,

A fire that burns all the day. Isaiah 65:5

Jesus is Lord of the universe yet "*He humbled himself and became obedient to the point of death, even the death of the cross*" (Phil 2:8) God did not think He was too holy to be around a bunch of sinful humans during his mortal life. He could have hung out with all the Pharisees because they were considered "holier" than everyone else. We cannot be like those Pharisees dancers. The type of dancers that think they are better than everyone else and think that participating in small events is beneath them; or they will not dance unless the venue has specific floors or lighting. We must be humble!

<u>Jesus was light.</u>

We must be in the world, but not part of the world. We must touch the world, but never turn to the world. We must change the world, but not cater to the world.

Then Jesus spoke to them again, saying, *"I am the light of the world. He who follows Me shall not walk in darkness, but have the light of life."*John 8:12

For you were once darkness, but now you are light in the Lord.

Walk as children of light

Eph 5:8

If you extend your soul to the hungry

And satisfy the afflicted soul,

Then your light shall dawn in the darkness,

And your darkness shall be as the noonday.

Isaiah 58:10

I do not have anything against official titles and positions or being part of an organized ministry. The house of the Lord should have order. I do not, however, agree when people refuse to work because they do not have a title. As if nothing could ever get done without a title. Leadership is not about position. You can be a ground breaking dancer, opening the doors to new and wonderful ways of praise and worship. You can inspire others not only to dance but to want to pursue their own ministry. When they see your passion, they will begin to want to pursue their own passion in ministry. You can do this and so much more without ever holding a title.

Jesus did not have a title nor did he care for one. Jesus did what God commanded him to do. I have a friend who was going to give up on their ministry because the leadership would not let them work or even help out. They were frustrated and did not want to deal with the drama anymore of practically begging to be part of it. That is the worst excuse I have ever heard. Never being given an official title is no excuse when standing in the presence of God and He asks you why you went and hid your talent. Nobody wants to accompany you to serve the needy? Go by yourself and volunteer at your local shelter. The choir director does not want to let you into the choir? Ask for your own participation and minister on your own. If nobody wants you to be part of their dance group? Find occasions to dance by yourself. Jesus performed miracles mostly on the streets. He did not wait until they invited him to come to a healing convention or saved his "best" sermons for the synagogue. His most known sermon was done outside on a mountain side and not in some fancy temple. If God has commanded you to do something than do it! You do not want to end up like the one servant who went off and hid his talent, waiting for the perfect time to invest. The time is now!

The Dance of Salome

On the opposite side of the spectrum, we have Salome. Salome was the daughter of Herodias and Phillip; step-daughter and niece to King Herod Antipas. John the Baptist was making a way and preaching good news throughout the land but when he rebuked King Herod, that his marriage to his brother's wife was unlawful, his wife became infuriated. The bible says that she nursed a grudge against him. Herodias, feeling offended and disrespected, encouraged Herod to capture and execute John the Baptist for his callus behavior. Herod feared what the people might do if he killed one of their prophets. He complied with his nagging wife and imprisoned John but refused to kill him.

I love how the scriptures describe this next part as a "convenient day" came; Convenient for whom? Convenient for Herodias and the plot she had formed against John. Herod's birthday had come and being the king that he is, he invited only the most important people to his party. He invited his high officials, military commanders, and all the leading men of Galilee. Herodias instructed her daughter, Salome, to dance before Herod and all his guests. Her dance pleased Herod so much that he vowed to give her anything she asked for, even half of his kingdom. Salome stepped out and went to her mother. She asked her what she thought she should ask for. Her mother advised her to ask for the beheading of John. The girl, instructed by her mother, went back to the kings party and asked for the head of John the Baptist on a platter. Herod felt like his back was against the wall. He did not want to kill John but he also could not back out on his promise, especially not in front of all his guests. He caved and sent the request to behead John the Baptist who was in prison. The head was brought to Salome on a platter and she then took it to her mother. (Matt 14:1-12; Mark 6:14-29)

Despite the horrendous way in which John the Baptist died, Salome is the epitome of how not to dance. Salome lacked in leadership and lacked a vision. Her dance was used for entertainment, seduction and manipulation. You can argue all day that it was her mother that was the evil one, and it was her mother that was at fault; but Salome was the one who danced and she was the one who made the request.

Divorced was not permitted back then. So in order for Herodias' marriage to be considered unlawful, she would have to have divorced her husband, seduce her brother in law and marry him. She had an agenda and that was to become queen. She did not care if she was breaking laws, much less hearts. Likewise, killing John the Baptist was only convenient for her and her agenda. Her behavior has a ghostly similarity to that of Jezebels; who is mostly remembered for seducing kings and killing prophets. Herodias seduced Herod into betraying his brother and marrying her. She already knew that seduction would work to manipulate him to get her way, but her seduction was powerless in this matter because Herod was a little stronger willed than Ahab (Jezebels Husband). So Herodias took drastic measures and used her daughter to dance in front of Herod and all his friends, who I am sure, were merry with wine; a.k.a. they were drunk. If you sleep with your brother's wife and then marry her while that brother is still alive, I think it is safe to say that your morals are pretty much non-existent. So, to also lust after you own niece is not all that far-fetched. Today, in modern times, if you hear that a woman went to a party and danced for a room full of drunken men, what would you assume her profession was? Exactly. Those women use their seduction to entertain and manipulate men into giving them what they want, which is usually money.

When we try to be "cool" or look "cute" while we dance, it gears the whole participation into a source of entertainment. We choreograph with the intent of being considered "cool", and only afterwards ask for God's anointing and to use us through movement. I have had the privilege to choreograph and every now and then I hear "I don't want to do that, because I don't feel cute doing it". Seriously? This is not an opportunity for you to show off how cute you think you are. We have to avoid ending up like Salome and dancing for entertainment purposes. I have also heard "We have to do this perfect because other churches are here and they can invite us to go dance for their events". That is not the reason you should want to do well; stop pimping your dance group out for exposure. Another comment I hear quite a bit is "Let's come up with really awesome choreography, so that more people will want to join the dance group". You are literally trying to seduce and manipulate people into join your ministry. There is way too much entertainment, seduction, and manipulation in our churches and not enough anointing.

Herodias represents our culture, our society, and the world whose main purpose is to destroy the church by any means necessary; and Salome, eager to please it. We cannot serve two masters. Fresh water and salt water cannot flow in the same river. The world is telling you to be cool and cute, but the Lord is telling you to be holy. When a praise dancer is only Christian by name and has not fully given their life to Christ, that person has no business dancing on the altar, much less not leading a ministry. We are so eager to please the requests of this world but refuse to consecrate our lives to Christ. Our mission is not to secularize the church; it is to take the gospel from church into the world. I do not have anything against training but there is a way to bring technique to praise dance without demoralizing the ministry. There is no doubt in my mind that Salome blamed her mother for her actions. The world can try to influence us all it wants, but not letting it affect us is a choice not a fortunate accident. When we are standing before the throne of God on judgment day, we cannot blame the media and society for our actions. God will respond with "No, it was you who danced and it was you who made the request, not your mother". We cannot let this world cloud our judgment.

Where there is no vision, the people perish:

but he that keepth the law, happy is he.

Pro 29:18 KJV

Salome lacked vision. The king was willing to grant her whatever she wanted but she decided to seek her mother, the world, to advise her on what she should ask for. Since she did not have a vision, she molded herself to whatever the world instructed her to. We need to develop visions for our ministries. We cannot just tumble like a leaf in the wind. What is the purpose of why we dance, and what do we want to achieve through our praise? We should always be striving toward a new goal and a new dream. We should be so connected with Christ that our heads are full of all these plans for the future on how to grow the kingdom through dance.

As a leader, you must have a plan of action. You must have a vision, purpose, and a mission for your ministry. A vision is "the act or power of anticipating that which will or may come to be". (6) A purpose is the reason for which mission exists. (7) A mission is an important assignment carried out for a purpose. (5) First, we must see where we are going; we cannot blindly walk aimlessly. We must, first, have a vision of where God wants to take us. In order to receive this vision from the Lord, we must be at one with Him. Next, there is the purpose. Why do are doing what you are doing? What is the goal you are trying to achieve? Then comes the mission, and this is the plan of action. How do you plan to get to the purpose? The vision is the what; the purpose is the why; and the mission is the how.

It does not have to be brain surgery or rocket science! God gave me a vision of me participating, teaching, writing and serving in the dance ministry. My purpose is to bring people to the feet of Jesus and to enlarge the kingdom with the gifts that He has given me. To showcase the awesomeness of God anytime I am given the opportunity; and preach the gospel in a way that only movement can deliver. My mission is to follow God's voice wherever it leads me, no matter how intimidating; So that He may use me at His will and to give all that I am over to him through prayer, fasting and a constant fellowship with Him. I explained what my vision was, why I do what I do, and how I plan on achieving it.

Beware the Golden Calf

Final Thoughts

Not that I have already attained, or am already perfected; but I

follow after,

if that I may apprehend that for which also I am apprehended of

Christ Jesus.

Brothers and sisters, I do not count myself to have apprehended; but

one thing

I do, forgetting those things which are behind and reaching forward

to those things

which are ahead, I press toward the mark for the prize of the high

calling of

God in Christ Jesus. but I press on, that I may lay hold of that for

which Christ

Jesus has also laid hold of me.

Phil 3:12-14 (NKJV, NLT, KJV)

I love that; it is one of my favorites! I did not write this book because I am so this and so that. I have not attained perfection as a dancer for the Kingdom but I strive toward it. Trying constantly to move forward and not going back to the person I once was; growing just a little every day. I am running towards the voice that is calling my name to work in His vineyard. I have not finished the race but I know that if I ever get tired of running, I can just continue walking. Never give up and sit on the side lines because it became too difficult, or walk back to the starting line. Striving to be as faithful and good as God has been with me.

I share with you what the Lord has revealed in my heart and the experiences that He has allowed me to live. So that it may bless you in knowledge and further your understanding of the ministry. Let us be kingdom minded! Not being selfish, a gossip, a hater, or a sneak in any way. Growing upwards towards heaven; growing fruit so that we may nourish and give shade to those who come to us. With roots that are so deep in Jesus and His gospel that no matter of wind could dig us up. Sure, a hurricane may come and blow all your leaves and some branches off; or a tornado can break you down to almost a stump; but if you remain rooted in the ground, you can grow again. Do not settle with being a dried up tree that has nothing to offer.

Let's grow as dancers! Let's grow the fruit of the spirit (love, joy, peace, patience, kindness, goodness, faithfulness, gentleness and self-control) our branches. Let's offer a good offering to God, so that we could make a difference in the world. We must grow underground in secret before we could grow into a tall and beautiful tree. Our nourishment comes mostly from the roots sucking the nutrients from the soil, more than from the sun. Nourish your spirit in privacy with the word, prayer and fasting; stop desiring the spotlight. Too much light will shrivel the plant. Have a desire to grow!

Work Cited

1 - http://bonasdancesite.homestead.com/Greek.html

2 - http://biblehub.com/topical/p/prochorus.htm

3 - https://www.google.com/webhp?sourceid=chrome-instant&ion=1&espv=2&ie=UTF-8#q=define+prophet

4- http://stronginfaith.org/article.php?page=90

5- https://search.yahoo.com/yhs/search?p=define+mission&ei=UTF-8&hspart=mozilla&hsimp=yhs-001

6 - http://dictionary.reference.com/browse/vision

7 - http://dictionary.reference.com/browse/purpose?s=t

Made in the USA
Middletown, DE
14 February 2018